SCOOBY-DOO!™

ON THE GO
Jokes!

by Michael Dahl
illustrated by Scott Jeralds

Starring...

Scooby-Doo!

Raintree is an imprint of Capstone Global Library Limited, a company incorporated in England and Wales having its registered office at 7 Pilgrim Street, London, EC4V 6LB – Registered company number: 6695582

www.raintree.co.uk
myorders@raintree.co.uk

CAPG34345

Edited by James Benefield and Eliza Leahy
Designed by Bob Lentz
Original illustrations © Hanna-Barbera 2015
Illustrated by Scott Jeralds
Production by Gene Bentdahl
Printed in China by Nordica
0914/CA21401580

ISBN 978-1-4062-9242-8 (paperback)
18 17 16 15 14
10 9 8 7 6 5 4 3 2 1

British Library Cataloguing in Publication Data
A full catalogue record for this book is available from the British Library.

Acknowledgements
Every effort has been made to contact copyright holders of material reproduced in this book. Any omissions will be rectified in subsequent printings if notice is given to the publisher.

All the Internet addresses (URLs) given in this book were valid at the time of going to press. However, due to the dynamic nature of the Internet, some addresses may have changed, or sites may have changed or ceased to exist since publication. While the author and publisher regret any inconvenience this may cause readers, no responsibility for any such changes can be accepted by either the author or the publisher.

Set List:

Bit one:
Where to?   **6**

Bit two:
Hit the ground running   **14**

Bit three:
Come on in! The water's fine!   **18**

Bit four:
Road trip!   **24**

Bit five:
Have jokes, will travel!   **34**

Bit six:
Airborne!   **42**

Bit seven:
Holiday time!   **46**

Bit eight:
A weird, weird world   **50**

Bit nine:
What d'ya say?   **54**

How to tell jokes!   58
More fun stuff   60

What do you call a city where there are no people?
Electri City.

Which is the cleverest country in the world?
Albania. It has three A's and one B!

Which European country has the least gravity?
No-weigh!

Why did the book go to the psychiatrist?
It kept talking to its shelf!

What do you call a snowman in Spain?
Water.

I hear Scooby might go to university.
Yes, he's been given a dog *collar*ship!

What is the coldest country in the world?
Chile.

LITTLE GIRL: I'd like to buy a plane ticket for Erwood.

TRAVEL AGENT: Erwood? Sorry, never heard of that. Where is Erwood?

LITTLE GIRL: He's over there. He's my brother.

Sorry, I can't go to the dance. I've sprained my ankle.

That's a *lame* excuse!

What do you call a giraffe at the North Pole?

Lost.

What stays in one corner but travels
around the world?
A stamp!

What do you call a fear of the North Pole?
Santa Claus-trophobia.

Bit two:
Hit the ground running

What should you always drink before a race?
Running water!

Have you heard about the runner who was afraid of hurdles?
He got over it.

Why did they throw Cinderella off of the netball team?
She kept running away from the ball!

Marathon runners can race for miles, and they only have to move **two feet!**

Why is the Mystery Inc. gang always so tired on the 1st of April?

Because they have just finished a march of 31 days!

A sloth went out for a walk and was mugged by a gang of snails. When he reported it to the police, the officer asked, "Can you describe the snails that attacked you?"

The sloth said, **"Sorry, it all happened so fast!"**

What does the winner of a race lose?
Her breath.

Have you heard about the two silkworms who had a race?
It ended in a tie.

Bit three:
Come on in!
The water's
fine!

What do you call little rivers in Egypt?
Juve-niles.

What happened when a red ship crashed
into a blue ship?
The crew was *marooned*!

Why do ferries have so many
angry people on board?
Because the boat makes them cross!

Where is the English Channel?
**I don't know. My TV doesn't
pick it up!**

What kind of stories are all about boats?
Ferry tales!

How do surfers greet each other?
They wave!

How do surfers clean themselves?
They wash up on shore!

What did Shaggy say to his friend while they were surfing?
"Scooby-Dude!"

Why are pirates called pirates?
Because they arrrrrrrr!

Shaggy went to the beach and sat down next to a sunbathing pig. Shaggy said, "It sure is hot." The pig said, **"You got that right. I'm bacon!"**

Is that boat expensive?
No, it's a sale-ing boat.

Where do you find *micro*waves?
On tiny little beaches!

How did the dentist cross the harbour?
He took the
Tooth Ferry!

What's the best day to go to the beach?
Sun-day!

How did the penguin cross the glacier?
He went with the floe.

Do you know where to find the Dead Sea?
Dead? I didn't even know it was ill!

Bit four:
Road trip!

What has four wheels and flies?
A dustbin lorry!

Why are you so late for school today?
The road sign outside says, "School ahead. Go slow."

What did Dorothy do when her dog got stuck on the yellow brick road?
She called the Toto truck!

Why did the cannibal drive on the motorway?
He heard the service stations were serving lorry drivers!

I don't think you should ever put a goldfish in a tank.

Everyone knows that fish can't drive!

What driver doesn't need a driving license?
A screwdriver!

Why don't you see the Mystery Machine parked outside football matches?
It's not a big sports van.

Have you heard about the magician who was driving down the road?

He turned into a driveway.

What's worse than raining cats and dogs?

Hailing taxis!

Why does an ambulance always have two medical experts on board?
Because they're a pair-a-medics.

What does a doctor take when she's feeling run down?
The registration number of the car that's just hit her!

What happens when a frog parks in a no-parking zone?
It gets toad away!

What kind of vehicle does a mad scientist drive?
A loco-motive!

How does a puppy carry luggage?
Easy, its little tail is a wagon.

Have you heard about the mechanic who slept under the car?

Yeah, he woke up *oily* the next morning.

When does a van stop working?
When it's re-tyred.

What do you call a laughing motorcycle?
A Yamahahaha!

What do you get when dinosaurs crash their cars?
Tyrannosaurus wrecks!

When does a van go to sleep?
When it's tyred.

Which snakes are found on cars?
Windscreen vipers!

Who has a job driving customers away?
A taxi driver.

Have you heard the joke about the dustbin lorry?
Don't worry. It's a load of rubbish.

Why did the Mystery Machine get a puncture?

There was a fork in the road!

What month do soldiers hate the most?
March!

What do you get when you cross a cowboy
with a map-maker?
A cow-tographer!

What lies on the ground, 100 feet in the air?
A dead centipede.

Shopping is good for helping you see the future!
It helps you see what's in store.

Wow! What a strange-looking painting.
It must be modern art!

Actually, Shaggy, that's a mirror.

Have you heard about the big game hunter who married the telephone operator?
Their lion is always busy!

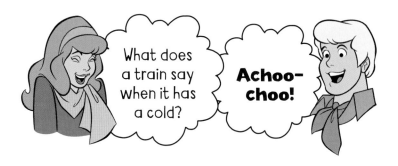

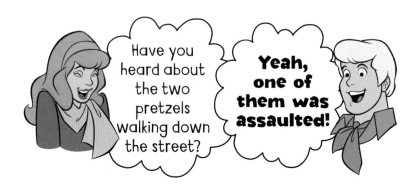

Have you heard about the two pretzels walking down the street?

Yeah, one of them was assaulted!

How do trains hear?
Through their engine-ears!

What's the difference between a teacher and a train conductor?
One trains the mind, and the other minds the train.

What is the difference between a well-dressed man on a tricycle and a poorly dressed man on a bicycle?
A-tyre!

CHILD: Doctor, my dog thinks he's an elevator!

DOCTOR: Then send him up to see me.

CHILD: I can't. He doesn't stop at this floor!

How do fleas travel from place to place?

They itch-hike!

Shaggy, why do you have two hair-curlers and two butter knives at the table?

I thought I'd make some roller-blades!

Why is it good to always travel with a barber?
They know all the short cuts!

Have you heard that Scooby fell into an upholstery machine?

Don't worry, he's fully re-covered!

Have you heard about the fire at the circus?

The heat was in tents!

Why can't the train play music?

It's on the wrong track.

I love staying at the hotel.

If you love it so much, why don't you Marriott?

What's the hardest part of skydiving?
The ground.

Why could the vulture only take two
dead badgers with him on the plane?
**Because they were
considered *carrion* items.**

What only starts to work after it's fired?
A rocket!

Why did the police officer arrest the balloon?

It broke the law of gravity.

What happens when you throw a clock in the air?
Time's up!

Scooby wondered why the boomerang kept getting bigger...
...then it finally hit him

What do you get if you cross a dog and an aeroplane?
A jet setter!

Bit seven:
Holiday time!

Where do locksmiths go on holiday?
The Florida Keys.

Where do buffalo go on holiday?
Rome.

Where do sharks go on holiday?
Finland.

Where do bacteria go on holiday?
Germany.

Where do lumps of sugar go on holiday?
Sweeten!

Where do knots go on holiday?
Tie-land.

Why did the boxer have an awful holiday?
All he packed was a punch!

Where did the worm go on holiday?
The Big Apple.

What do you call a piece of paper that
doesn't go anywhere?
Stationary stationery.

Bit eight:
A weird, weird world

Which is the world's laziest mountain?
Everest.

Which is the thirstiest body of water in the world?
The Gulp of Mexico!

Where can you find the Great Plains?
At great airports!

Which is the fastest country in the world?
Russia.

Why is the Equator boiling mad?
Because it's 360 degrees!

Which statue stands in New York,
holds a torch and sneezes?
**The *Atchoo!* of
Liberty.**

What's a light year?
**The same as a normal year, but
with fewer calories.**

Which is the wettest country
in the world?

The United Kingdom.
The queen has
reigned for
over 60 years!

Bit nine:
What d'ya say?

What did one escalator say to the other?
"I think I'm *coming down* with something."

What did the rucksack say to the hat?
"You go on ahead, I'll go on back."

What did the cowboy say after he was thrown off his horse?
"I've fallen and I can't giddy-up!"

What did the tornado say to the sports car?
"Want to go for a spin?"

What did the jack say to the car?
"Can I give you a lift?"

What did one traffic light say to the other traffic light?
"Don't look! I'm changing!"

What do you say to a cow that walks in front of your car?
"Mooo-ve over!"

What did the sleeping bag say to the Scout?
"I've got you covered!"

What did the toadstool say when it moved into its new house?
"Not mushroom in here!"

What did one volcano say to the other?
"I lava you!"

What do you say to a frog who needs a lift?
"Hop in!"

How to Tell Jokes!

1. KNOW the joke
Make sure you remember the whole joke before you tell it. This sounds obvious, but most of us know someone who says, "Oh, this is so funny..." Then, when they tell the joke, they can't remember the end. And that's the whole point of a joke – its punchline.

2. SPEAK CLEARLY
Don't mumble: don't speak too quickly or too slowly. Just speak like you normally do. You don't have to use a different voice or accent or sound like someone else. (UNLESS that's part of the joke!)

3. LOOK at your audience
Good eye contact with your listeners will grab their attention.

4. DON'T WORRY about gestures or how to stand or sit when you tell your joke. Remember, telling a joke is basically talking.

5. DON'T LAUGH at your own joke
Yeah, yeah, I know some comedians crack up while they're acting in a sketch or telling a story, but the best rule to follow is not to laugh. If you start to laugh, you might lose the rhythm of your joke or stop yourself from telling the joke clearly. Let your audience laugh. That's their job. Your job is to be the funny one.

6. THE PUNCHLINE is the most important part of the joke
It's the climax, the reward, the main event. A good joke can sound even better if you pause for just a second or two before you deliver the punchline. That tiny pause will make your audience mentally sit up and hold their breath, eager to hear what's coming next.

7. The SETUP is the second most important part of a joke

That's basically everything you say before you get to the punchline. And that's why you need to be as clear as you can (see 2 on the opposite page) so that when you finally reach the punchline, it makes sense!

8. YOU CAN GET FUNNIER

It's easy. Watch other comedians. Listen to other people tell a joke or story. Go and see a good comedy show or film. You can pick up some skills simply by seeing how others get their comedy across. You will absorb it! And soon it will come naturally.

9. Last, but not least, telling a joke is all about TIMING

That means not only getting the biggest impact for your joke, waiting for the right time, giving that extra pause before the punchline – but it also means knowing when NOT to tell a joke. When you're among friends, you can tell when they'd like to hear something funny. But in an unfamiliar setting, get a "sense of the room" first. Are people having a good time? Or is it a more serious event? A joke has the most funny power when it's told in the right setting.

How is **Michael Dahl** like a skyscraper?

They both have lots of stories!

Dahl has written more than two hundred stories for young readers. He is the author of *The Everything Kids' Joke Book*, *Laff-O-Tronic Joke Books*, the scintillating *Duck Goes Potty* and two humorous mystery series: Finnegan Zwake and Hocus Pocus Hotel. He has toured the United States with an improv troupe and began his auspicious comic career at primary school when his stand-up routine made his music teacher laugh so hard she fell off her chair. She is not available for comment.

How is **Scott Jeralds** different from a car radio?

One is full of 'toons, and the other is full of tunes!

Jeralds has worked in 'toons (animation) for companies including Marvel Studios, Hanna-Barbera Studios, M.G.M. Animation, Warner Bros. and Porchlight Entertainment. Scott has worked on TV series such as *The Flintstones*, *Yogi Bear*, *Scooby-Doo*, *The Jetsons*, *Krypto the Superdog*, *Tom and Jerry*, *The Pink Panther*, *Superman*, *Secret Saturdays* and he directed the cartoon series *Freakazoid*, for which he won an Emmy Award. In addition, Scott has designed cartoon-related merchandise, licensing art and artwork for several comic and children's book publications.

Joke Dictionary!

bit section of a comedy routine

comedian entertainer who makes people laugh

headliner last comedian to perform in a show

improvisation performance that hasn't been planned: "improv" for short

lineup list of people who are going to perform in a show

one-liner short joke or funny remark

open mike event at which anyone can use the microphone to perform for the audience

punchline words at the end of a joke that make it funny or surprising

shtick repetitive, comic performance or routine

segue sentence or phrase that leads from one joke or routine to another

stand-up type of comedy performed while standing alone on stage

timing use of rhythm and tempo to make a joke funnier

SCOOBY-DOO!

Joke Books!

Only from...
RAINTREE!

The fun doesn't stop here!

Discover more at...
raintree.co.uk